Milkshake Recipes

Creamy Delicious Milkshake Recipes with a Modern Twist

(The Most Delicious and Healthiest Milkshake Recipes)

Terrance Dandy

Published By **Tyson Maxwell**

Terrance Dandy

Milkshake Recipes: Creamy Delicious Milkshake Recipes with a Modern Twist (The Most Delicious and Healthiest Milkshake Recipes)

ISBN   978-1-990373-71-8

Legal & Disclaimer

Upon using the information contained in this book, you agree to hold harmless the Author from and against any damages, costs, and expenses, including any legal fees potentially resulting from the application of any of the information provided by this guide. This disclaimer applies to any damages or injury caused by the use and application, whether directly or indirectly, of any advice or information presented, whether for breach of contract, tort, negligence, personal injury, criminal intent, or under any other cause of action.

You agree to accept all risks of using the information presented inside this book. You need to consult a professional medical practitioner in order to ensure you are both able and healthy enough to participate in this program.

Table of Contents

Chapter 1: Non-Alcoholic

Recipe 1: Triple Strawberry Shake

If you're crazy for strawberry, then you'll simply adore this triple berry shake with strawberry flavored ice cream, sorbet, and preserves! A splash of lemon juice helps to balance the sweetness.

Makes: 2-3

Preparation Time: 10mins

Ingredient List:

- 4 scoops each strawberry ice cream and strawberry sorbet (softened)
- ½ cup skim milk
- 2 tablespoons strawberry preserves
- 1 teaspoon lemon juice.

Instructions:

1. Add the ice cream, sorbet, milk, preserves, and lemon juice in a blender and blitz until smooth.

2. Pour into glasses and serve straight away.

Recipe 2: Matcha Green Tea Malts

Adding matcha to desserts and treats has been one of the biggest food trends of 2017. Get in on the buzz with these yummy matcha green tea malted milkshakes.

Makes: 1-2

Preparation Time: 5mins

Ingredient List:

- ½ cup skim milk
- 1¼ cups vanilla bean ice cream
- 1 tablespoon matcha green tea powder
- 1½ tablespoons malt powder

- 1-2 drops vanilla essence
- 2 teaspoons organic honey

Instructions:

1. Add the milk, ice cream, matcha, malt powder, vanilla essence, and honey into a blender. Blitz until smooth and pour into a large glass.

2. Serve immediately.

Recipe 3: Coffee and Donut Milkshakes

Coffee and donuts go together like peanut butter and jelly, which makes them the perfect inspiration for a creamy and indulgent milkshake.

Makes: 2-3

Preparation Time: 5mins

Ingredient List:

- 1 cup ice coffee
- 1 cup skim milk

- 2 cups coffee flavor ice cream
- 1 cup vanilla flavor ice cream
- 2 plain ring donuts
- Ice

Instructions:

1. Add the ice coffee, milk, ice creams and donuts into a blender along with a small handful of ice. Blitz until smooth.

2. Pour into glasses and serve immediately.

Recipe 4: Mango Madness

With fresh ripe mango, this fruit milkshake is bursting with tropical flavor.

Makes: 3-4

Preparation Time: 10mins

Ingredient List:

- 3 ripe mangoes (peeled, pitted, chopped)
- 3 cups whole milk
- Sugar to taste

Instructions:

1. Add the mango and milk to a blender, blitz until smooth. Taste, and add sugar until you reach your desired level of sweetness.

2. Pour into ice-filled glasses and serve immediately.

Recipe 5: Banana Cream Pudding

Milkshake

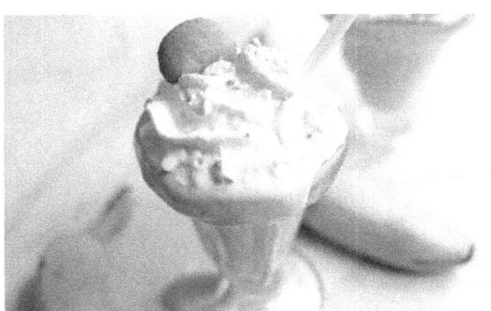

Thick and packed full of big banana flavor, this scrummy milkshake is like pudding in a glass.

Makes: 1

Preparation Time: 5mins

Ingredient List:

- ¾ cup whole milk
- 3 teaspoons instant banana pudding mix
- 1 cup vanilla frozen yogurt
- 5 vanilla wafer cookies

Instructions:

1. Add the whole milk and banana pudding mix into a blender and blitz until smooth.

2. Add the frozen yogurt and blend again until well incorporated.

3. Crumble in the wafer cookies and blend until the shake is lump-free.

Recipe 6: White Wedding Cake

Milkshakes

This milkshake literally tastes like liquid wedding cake; the secret is the addition of a scoop of white cake batter mix. We won't tell if you don't!

Makes: 2-3

Preparation Time: 10mins

Ingredient List:

- 1½ cups sweet coffee creamer
- ½ cup boxed white cake mix

- 3 scoops vanilla ice cream
- ½ cup ice
- Skim milk

Instructions:

1. Add the coffee creamer, white cake mix, ice cream and ice in a blender. Blitz until smooth. Add milk a splash at a time until you achieve a consistency that can be drunk through a straw.

2. Pour into glasses and serve straight away.

Recipe 7: Brown Butter and Peach

Milkshakes

The key to the delicious flavor of this heavenly milkshake is the fresh ripe peaches, cooked in browned butter and sugar.

Makes: 2

Preparation Time: 1hour 45mins

Ingredient List:

- 3 tablespoons unsalted butter
- 2 tablespoons brown sugar

- 2 ripe peaches (pitted, sliced)
- 1 cup skim milk
- 4 scoops vanilla ice cream
- 4 vanilla sandwich cookies (crumbled)

Instructions:

1. Melt the butter in a skillet over moderate heat. Cook for 3-4 minutes until browned. Add the sugar and stir before adding the peaches. Cook for 6-8 minutes, turning the slices over halfway. Take off the heat and set to one side to cool.

2. Add the skim milk, vanilla ice cream, any remaining butter from the skillet, and cooled peaches. Blitz until smooth.

3. Pour into two tall glasses and sprinkle the crumbled cookies equally over each.

Recipe 8: Toasted Coconut and Vanilla

Milkshake

Toasting the coconut before blending gives this tropical milkshake a deeper and more intense coconutty flavor.

Makes: 2

Preparation Time: 35mins

Ingredient List:

- 1 cup shredded coconut
- 2 cups vanilla flavor frozen yogurt

- 3 cups vanilla flavor coconut milk

Instructions:

1. In a pan over low-moderate heat, toast the coconut until fragrant and brown, tossing occasionally to ensure it doesn't catch. Set aside for 15 minutes to cool.

2. Add the toasted coconut, frozen yogurt, and coconut milk to a blender. Blitz until smooth and pour into glasses.

3. Enjoy immediately.

Recipe 9: Cake Batter Shakes

If you're one of those people that can't resist licking the bowl clean when baking, then this is the shake for you!

Makes: 2

Preparation Time: 5mins

Ingredient List:

- 2 cups vanilla ice cream
- 1 cup semi skim milk
- ½ cup funfetti boxed cake mix

- Hundreds and thousands

Instructions:

1. Add the ice cream, skim milk, and cake mix into a blender and blitz until smooth.

2. Pour into two tall glasses and scatter over hundreds and thousands before serving.

Recipe 10: Tiramisu Milkshakes

With iced mocha coffee, mascarpone cheese, ladyfinger cookies and vanilla ice cream, this is one sophisticated milkshake that the grownups will appreciate!

Makes: 2

Preparation Time: 10mins

Ingredient List:

- 4 scoops vanilla bean ice cream
- ½ cup iced mocha coffee
- 2 tablespoons mascarpone cheese
- 2 ladyfinger biscuits
- Whole milk
- Whip cream
- Cocoa powder

Instructions:

1. Add the ice cream, iced coffee, mascarpone cheese, and biscuits into a blender. Blitz until smooth. Add milk a splash at a time until the milkshake is a drinkable consistency.

2. Top each portion with whip cream and dust with cocoa powder.

Recipe 11: Cheesecake Shakes

All the flavor of a big wedge of sweet and tangy cheesecake in a slurpable shake.

Makes: 3

Preparation Time: 5mins

Ingredient List:

- 4 ounces full-fat cream cheese (chilled, chopped)

- 6 scoop good quality vanilla ice cream
- ⅔ cup whole milk
- 1 tablespoon crumbed graham crackers
- Whip cream
- 3 maraschino cherries

Instructions:

1. Add the cream cheese, ice cream, whole milk and crumbed graham crackers into a blender. Blitz until smooth.

2. Pour into glasses. Top each with whip cream and a maraschino cherry.

3. Serve immediately.

Recipe 12: Sweet 'n Salty Peanut Butter

Milkshakes

Our two favorite salty 'n sweet treats; peanut butter and salted caramel, all in one out of this world milkshake.

Makes: 2

Preparation Time: 5mins

Ingredient List:

- 3 cups vanilla bean ice cream
- ¼ cup smooth peanut butter
- ¼ cup salted caramel sauce
- 2 teaspoons vanilla essence
- 8 tablespoons sugar
- 2 cups whole milk

Instructions:

1. Add the ice cream, peanut butter, caramel sauce, vanilla, sugar and whole milk in a blender. Blitz until smooth and pour into tall glasses.

2. Enjoy straight away,

Recipe 13: Classic Pistachio Nut Milkshake

Sometimes you just can't beat the classics, like this well-loved pistachio flavored milkshake made with real whole nuts.

Makes: 2

Preparation Time: 7mins

Ingredient List:

- 24 raw pistachios (shelled)
- 6-8 scoops pistachio choc chunk ice cream
- Whole milk
- Whip cream
- Dark chocolate (shaved)

Instructions:

1. In a blender, add the nuts and ice cream. Blitz until smooth and lump free. Add the milk a little at a time until you achieve a consistency that is drinkable through a straw.

2. Pour into tall glasses and top each with a dollop of whip cream. Sprinkle with grated chocolate.

3. Serve immediately.

Recipe 14: Shamrock Shake Recipe

Celebrating St.Patrick's day, feeling patriotic, or just really love peppermint flavored treats; this fun and tasty shake is perfect for any occasion.

Makes: 2

Preparation Time: 8mins

Ingredient List:

- 3 cups vanilla bean ice cream
- 1¾ cups semi skim milk
- ½ teaspoons peppermint essence
- Few drops green food gel

- Whip cream
- Green maraschino cherries (for garnish)

Instructions:

1. Add the ice cream; semi skim milk and peppermint essence into a blender. Blitz until smooth. Blend in the food gel a drop at a time until you reached your desired shade of shamrock green.

2. Pour into glasses. Top each with a dollop of whip cream and garnish each with a green cherry.

Recipe 15: Cotton Candy Milkshake

A super fun milkshake made with real cotton candy that will make you feel like a big kid again!

Makes: 1-2

Preparation Time: 5mins

Ingredient List:

- 1½ cups classic pink cotton candy
- 4 scoops cotton candy flavor ice cream
- 1 teaspoon vanilla essence
- ½ cup skim milk

Instructions:

1. In a blender, add the cotton candy, ice cream, vanilla essence, and skim milk. Blitz until smooth and pour into a tall glass.

2. Serve immediately.

Recipe 16: Snickerdoodle Milkshake

A cinnamon spiced milkshake made with real snickerdoodle cookies is just what the doctor ordered after a long, difficult day.

Makes: 2

Preparation Time: 7mins

Ingredient List:

- 3 cups vanilla bean ice cream
- ¾ cup semi skim milk
- ¾ teaspoons ground cinnamon
- 4 (3") leftover snickerdoodle cookies (crumbled)

Instructions:

1. Add the ice cream; semi skim milk, cinnamon, and ¾ of the crumbled cookies into a blender. Blitz until smooth.

2. Pour into glasses. Sprinkle the remaining cookie pieces equally over each portion.

3. Serve!

Recipe 17: Double Chocolate Red Velvet

Milkshakes

With two types of choc chips, ice cream, chocolate milk, and whole red velvet cupcakes, this is one monster milkshake that is not to be missed.

Makes: 1-2

Preparation Time: 5mins

Ingredient List:

- 1 cup chocolate flavor milk
- 2 cups vanilla bean ice cream
- 2 unfrosted red velvet cupcakes
- 1 tablespoon semisweet choc chips
- 1 tablespoon white choc chips

- 2 tablespoons chocolate flavor ice cream sauce
- Whip cream (for topping)

Instructions:

1. Add the milk, ice cream, cupcakes, choc chips and chocolate sauce in a blender and blitz until smooth,

2. Pour into a large glass and top with a generous dollop of whip cream,

3. Serve immediately.

Recipe 18: Salted Caramel Mocha Ice

Cream Milkshake

Salted caramel, coffee, chocolate, and ice cream!? Literally, all of our favorite things in one tall glass.

Makes: 1

Preparation Time: 10mins

Ingredient List:

- ¼ cup whole milk
- 1 scoop chocolate ice cream
- 3 tablespoons chocolate flavor ice cream sauce
- ¼ cup strongly brewed coffee (chilled)

- Salted caramel sauce
- 1 scoop vanilla ice cream

Instructions:

1. Add the whole milk, chocolate ice cream, sauce, and coffee in a blender. Blitz until smooth.

2. Take a tall glass; generously drizzle salted caramel sauce into the glass so that all sides are coated until dripping.

3. Pour the milkshake into the glass and top with a scoop of vanilla ice cream.

4. Serve straight away.

Recipe 19: Earl Grey and Honey

Milkshakes

Earl Grey is a delicate floral tea with hints of bergamot and orange; the flavors pair perfectly with raw honey.

Makes: 2

Preparation Time: 1hour 15mins

Ingredient List:

- 2 bags Earl Grey tea
- ½ cup boiling hot water
- 2 tablespoons raw honey
- 1½ cups vanilla bean ice cream
- 1 cup skim milk
- ½ cup cream
- Whip cream (for topping)

- Honey (for drizzling)

Instructions:

1. Steep the tea in the hot water for 4-5 minutes. Squeeze the tea bags and discard. Dissolve the honey in the hot tea. Chill until cool.

2. In a blender, blitz together the cooled tea, vanilla ice cream, skim milk, and cream until smooth.

3. Pour into glasses. Top with whip cream and finish with a drizzle of honey.

Recipe 20: Purple Cow Shakes

Little ones will go crazy for these bright purple shakes flavored with grape juice and thickened with creamy vanilla ice cream.

Makes: 2-3

Preparation Time: 10mins

Ingredient List:

- 6 ounces frozen grape juice concentrate
- 2 cups vanilla ice cream
- 1 cup semi skim milk

Instructions:

1. Add the juice concentrate, ice cream, and skim milk into a blender. Blitz until smooth.

2. Pour into tall glasses and enjoy straight away!

Recipe 21: Fresh Fig and Banana

Milkshake

If you love milkshakes but are looking for something a little lighter, why not try this healthier alternative; made with fresh fig, banana, and sweetened with honey.

Makes: 2

Preparation Time: 5mins

Ingredient List:

- 8 fresh ripe pigs (peeled)
- 1 ripe banana (peeled, chopped)
- 1 cup almond milk
- 1 cup vanilla ice cream
- ½ teaspoons raw honey

Instructions:

1. In a blender, add the figs, banana, milk, ice cream and honey. Blitz until smooth, taste and add a little more honey if you would like a sweeter flavor. Pour into tall glasses.

2. Serve immediately.

Recipe 22: Pumpkin Pie Milkshakes

Planning a holiday party? Then these festive little milkshakes flavored with real pumpkin pie and spices are a must.

Makes: 8-10 (small shakes)

Preparation Time: 10mins

Ingredient List:

- 1½ cups vanilla ice cream
- 1 cup leftover pumpkin pie (broken into pieces)

- ⅔ cup whole milk
- ¼ teaspoons pumpkin pie spice
- Whip cream
- Cinnamon sticks

Instructions:

1. Add the ice cream, crumbled pie, whole milk, and spice into a blender and blitz until smooth,

2. Pour into serving glasses. Top each with a dollop of whip cream and garnish with a cinnamon stick.

3. Serve immediately.

Recipe 23: Grilled Pineapple Tiki Shakes

Grilling the pineapple before blending, gives these tiki shakes a more complex and interesting flavor.

Makes: 2

Preparation Time: 1hour 30mins

Ingredient List:

- ½ fresh medium pineapple (peeled, cored, chopped into 2" chunks)
- 2 teaspoons coconut oil
- 1 pint coconut milk vanilla flavor ice cream
- Splash milk

Instructions:

1. Preheat the main oven to 350 degrees F. Line a baking sheet with parchment.

2. Toss the pineapple chunks in the coconut oil and arrange on the baking sheet.

3. Place in the oven and roast for half an hour, flipping the fruit halfway through cooking. Set aside to cool.

4. Add the cooled pineapple, vanilla ice cream, and splash of milk in a blender. Blitz until combined.

5. Pour into tall glasses and serve.

Recipe 24: Mexican Spiced Chocolate

Milkshakes

A fudgy homemade Mexican chocolate sauce forms the base of these wickedly indulgent milkshakes.

Makes: 2

Preparation Time: 1hour 25mins

Ingredient List:

Chocolate sauce:

- 1½ rounds (from a 2.7 ounce packet) Mexican chocolate
- 1 cup heavy cream

Milkshake:

- 2 cups vanilla bean ice cream
- ½ cup Mexican chocolate sauce
- Splash milk
- Handful candy shell coated chocolates (crushed)

Instructions:

1. Add the Mexican chocolate and heavy cream into a saucepan over a moderate heat. Cook while whisking until the chocolate melts into the cream. Set aside to cool.

2. Add the ice cream and half a cup of the chocolate sauce into a blender. Blitz until smooth. Add a little milk at a time to loosen the consistency until drinkable through a straw.

3. Pour into tall glasses and sprinkle over crushed candies.

4. Serve immediately.

Recipe 25: Lemon Cream Pie Milkshakes

When temperatures soar, we'll be enjoying our favorite baked treats in drink form!

Makes: 4

Preparation Time: 10mins

Ingredient List:

- ½ cup organic lemon curd
- 1½ cups whole milk
- Whip cream
- 3 cups vanilla ice cream
- 4 sugar/shortbread cookies (crumbled)
- Sliced lemon (for rim)

Instructions:

1. Add the lemon curd, ice cream, and milk in a blender Blitz until super smooth.

2. Pour into the glasses and top each with a dollop of whip cream, sprinkle the crumbled cookies over evenly and garnish each glass with a slice of lemon.

Chapter 2: Alcoholic

Recipe 26: Coffee with a Creamy Kick

What a wake- up call!

Makes: 1

Preparation Time: 2mins

Ingredient List:

- 1 cup coffee ice cream
- ⅓ cup whole milk
- 1 ounce coffee liqueur

Instructions:

1. Combine the ice cream with the milk and liqueur in a food blender and blitz until silky smooth.

Recipe 27: White Chocolate Peppermint Milkshake

A popular holiday drink or shake, to enjoy at any time of the year.

Makes: 2

Preparation Time: 5mins

Ingredient List:

- ¼ cup white chocolate flavor liqueur
- 2 cups peppermint ice cream
- ¼ cup heavy whipping cream
- Whip cream (to garnish)
- Candy cane (to garnish)

Instructions:

1. Add the liqueur, ice cream and whipping cream into a blender and process until silky smooth.

2. If the drink is too thick, then use more cream to thin it out.

3. Top with whip cream and a few candy canes.

4. Serve.

Recipe 28: Banana Cream Rumshake

Rum and banana is a culinary marriage made in heaven, so whip up this shake whenever you need to spoil yourself.

Makes: 1-2

Preparation Time: 4mins

Ingredient List:

- 1½ ounces white rum
- 1½ ounces crème de banane
- 1 tablespoon instant banana pudding mix
- 4 scoops vanilla ice- cream

- Cold milk

Instructions:

1. In a food blender, combine the rum, crème de banana and banana pudding mix and process until the pudding mix is dissolved and the ingredients are combined.

2. Add the vanilla ice cream and blitz until silky.

3. Add cold milk a little at a time until you achieve your desired consistency.

4. Serve in a tall chilled glass and enjoy.

Recipe 29: The Green Goddess

Fresh and minty, the perfect drink for St.Patrick's Day maybe?

Makes: 1-2

Preparation Time: 5mins

Ingredient List:

For mint syrup:

- 1 cup sugar
- 1 cup cold water
- 1 small bunch (1 cup) fresh mint

Shake:

- 2½ cups vanilla ice cream
- ¼ cup whole milk
- 3 ounces Irish whiskey
- ¼ teaspoons mint essence
- 4-6 drops green food coloring
- 2 drops yellow food coloring

Toppings:

- Whipped cream
- Maraschino cherries

Instructions:

1. First, make the syrup: In a pan heat the sugar, water, and mint leaves. Heat until the sugar is dissolved.

2. Transfer the mint syrup to a heat-safe bowl and transfer to the fridge to cool, for around 20 minutes.

3. Strain the mint, over a clean bowl, and discard the mint leaves. Put 2 tablespoons of mint syrup aside for your shake and put the rest to one side for another purpose.

4. Combine the 2 tablespoons of syrup with the ice cream, whole milk, Irish whiskey, mint essence and the food colorings. Blend until silky smooth and serve.

Recipe 30: Best Butterscotch Boozy Shake

Bring on the butter with this butter pecan and butterscotch flavored boozy beverage.

Makes: 1-2

Preparation Time: 4mins

Ingredient List:

- 3 large scoops butter pecan ice cream
- ½ cup whole milk (divided)
- 2 ounces butterscotch schnapps
- Whip cream (to garnish)
- Butterscotch ice cream topping (to garnish)

Instructions:

1. Chill two short glasses in the freezer.

2. In a food blender, combine the ice cream with half of the milk, and process until combined. Add more milk if necessary.

3. Add the schnapps and stir to incorporate.

4. Divide between the two chilled glasses and garnish with whip cream and a drizzle of butterscotch ice cream topping.

Recipe 31: Single Malt S'mores Milkshake

Here's one for Burns' Night, a single malt shake made with chocolate ice cream and served in a glass rimmed with caramel and crackers.

Makes: 2

Preparation Time: 7mins

Ingredient List:

- 1 pint chocolate ice cream
- ½ cup whole milk
- ⅓ cup single malt scotch
- 6 roasted marshmallows (divided)
- 2 teaspoons caramel
- 3 tablespoons graham crackers (crushed)
- Whipped cream

Instructions:

1. Add the chocolate ice cream, along with the whole milk, Scotch and 4 marshmallows to a food blender, and slowly blend until silky smooth.

2. Lightly rim each of your glasses with caramel.

3. Put the cracker crumbs in a shallow dish and dip the caramel rims into the crumbs, making sure they are evenly coated.

4. Pour the milkshake into each glass and garnish with whipped cream.

5. Sprinkle with the remaining crumbs and add finally add a marshmallow to each glass.

Recipe 32: Boozy Berry Chocolate Almond

Milkshake

Berries and chocolate pair perfectly with rum and amaretto, add a dollop of whipped cream, and you have an indulgent and decadent drink or dessert.

Makes: 2

Preparation Time: 22mins

Ingredient List:

- 2 cups berries (of choice)
- ¼ cup sugar

- 3 cups chocolate ice cream
- ¼ cup whole milk
- 2 ounces dark rum
- 1 ounce amaretto
- 2 teaspoons pure chocolate extract
- 1 teaspoon almond extract
- Whipped cream (for garnish)
- Sliced almonds (for garnish)
- Cacao nibs (for garnish)

Instructions:

1. Add the berries along with the sugar to a pot placed over moderate to low heat, and cook for 12-15 minutes, until syrupy. Puree the mixture and using a fine mesh sieve, strain out and discard any seeds.

2. Add the chocolate ice cream, along with the whole milk, dark rum, and amaretto, followed by the chocolate extract, and almond extract to a food blender and process until silky smooth.

3. Pour the berry puree between 2 tall glasses and swirl to coat.

4. Add the milkshake and garnish with whipped cream, sliced almonds, and cacao nibs.

5. Serve.

Recipe 33: Pretty n Pink Birthday Drink

Make sure you put a couple of chunks of birthday cake to one side. When the clearing up is finished spoil yourself with this after party shake.

Makes: 1-2

Preparation Time: 2mins

Ingredient List:

- 2 ounces vanilla vodka
- 3 scoops strawberry ice cream
- Dash of whole milk

- Ice cubes
- Simple syrup (to rim)
- Pink sprinkles (to rim)

Toppings:

- Whipped cream
- 2 medium size cubes birthday cake
- Few fresh strawberries

Instructions:

1. In a food blender, blend the vodka along with the ice cream, a dash of milk and a few ice cubes. Add additional ice cream for thickness, or a drop more milk to thin the consistency out.

2. Line the rim of each glass with simple syrup and pink sprinkles.

3. Pour your shake into a tall glass and garnish with whipped cream, birthday cake, and fresh strawberries.

Recipe 34: Boozy Unicorn Milkshakes

An over 21 version of a unicorn milkshake to bring out your inner child.

Makes: 2

Preparation Time: 10mins

Ingredient List:

- 8 ounces vanilla ice cream
- ¼ whole cup milk
- 3-4 ounces vodka (to taste)
- Pink food coloring
- Blue food coloring

Toppings:

- Whipped cream
- Mini marshmallows

- Rainbow sprinkles

Instructions:

1. In a food blender, process the ice cream together with the whole milk and vodka, until you achieve your preferred consistency.

2. Evenly divide the shake between 2 jugs.

3. Color one with pink food coloring and the other with blue food coloring.

4. Take two chilled Champagne flutes. Fill each glass halfway with the pink shake and top up with the blue milkshake.

5. Garnish with whipped cream, mini mallows, and rainbow sprinkles.

Recipe 35: Limoncello Milkshake

An Italian inspired milkshake; so, good it could almost be a dessert.

Makes: 2-4

Preparation Time: 3mins

Ingredient List:

- 1 pint ice cream
- 3 shots limoncello
- ½ cup whole milk
- 1 cup ice

Instructions:

1. In a food blender, process the ice cream, limoncello, whole milk, and ice.

2. Add a drop more milk if the shake is too thick, or ice cream to thicken.

3. Enjoy.

Recipe 36: Bourbon Spiked Pumpkin Pie

Shake

A little goes a long way with this delicious pumpkin inspired shake so enjoy responsibly!

Makes: 2-3

Preparation Time: 4mins

Ingredient List:

- Honey (to rim)
- Edible gold sprinkles (to rim)
- 3 cups vanilla ice cream
- ½ cup whole milk
- ¼ cup cream
- 1 tablespoon pure vanilla extract
- ½ cup pumpkin puree
- 2 teaspoons pumpkin pie spice
- ½ teaspoons cinnamon
- ¼ cup graham cracker (crumbs)
- 3 ounces bourbon
- Cinnamon (to garnish)

Instructions:

1. Rim each glass with honey, and dip each rim in the gold sprinkles, twisting to ensure they are evenly coated. Set the glasses to one side.

2. Add the ice cream, milk, cream, vanilla extract, pumpkin puree, pumpkin pie spice, cinnamon, graham cracker crumbs and bourbon in a food blender, and blend until silky smooth and combined.

3. Evenly divide the shake between the glasses.

4. Garnish with cinnamon and serve.

Recipe 37: Lavender and White Chocolate

Boozy Milkshakes

Fragrant and sweet, a vodka-based boozy shake.

Makes: 4

Preparation Time: 1hour 20mins*

Ingredient List:

Infused vodka:

- ¾ cup vodka
- 1 tablespoon culinary lavender

Milkshake:

- 1 cup half & half
- 1 tablespoon culinary lavender
- 4 ounces white chocolate (chopped)
- 8 cups vanilla ice cream

Instructions:

1. For the vodka infusion: In a Mason jar, combine the vodka along with the culinary lavender. Seal and allow the infusion to rest for between 1½ -2 days, at room temperature.

2. Strain the mixture, over a clean bowl and discard the lavender.

3. Next, make the half & half infusion. In a pan over moderate heat, warm the half & half along with the lavender until bubbles begin to form, without allowing the mixture to boil.

4. Remove the pan from the heat, cover with a lid, and allow the mixture to rest for half an hour. Next, strain, into a clean bowl and discard the lavender.

5. Return the half & half infusion to the pan and add the white chocolate.

6. Gently warm over a low to moderate heat, frequently stirring, until the chocolate is melted. Remove the pan from the heat and set to one side to cool.

7. Next, make the shakes.

8. To a food, blender add 2 cups of ice cream, 3 tablespoons of infused vodka, and ¼ cup of the half and half-chocolate mixture and process on high speed until silky smooth.

9. Pour into a tall glass and enjoy.

10. Repeat the process another three times until you have four servings.

*Plus approximately two days infusion time.

Recipe 38: Chilled Buttered Rum Shake

Pecan pie in a glass, a spicy rum treat to share with friends.

Makes: 2-3

Preparation Time: 6mins

Ingredient List:

- ½ cup whole milk
- 3 tablespoons amber rum
- 3 tablespoons light brown sugar
- Pinch ground cloves
- Pinch freshly grated nutmeg
- 8 scoops butter pecan ice cream

Instructions:

1. Add the whole milk, amber rum, brown sugar, ground cloves and nutmeg in a food blender and blitz to incorporate, for around 20 seconds.

2. Add the butter pecan ice cream and pulse 5-6 times to break the ice cream up.

3. While the blender is still running and using a rubber spatula, carefully push the mixture down the blades.

4. Continue to plus, stop, and mash until the milkshake is blended, thickened but easily moves around in the food blender jug.

5. Divided between chilled Collins glasses and serve.

Recipe 39: Cookies, Cream, and Coconut

Rum

Ahoy, there mateys! A rum infused milkshake is perfect to chill out with.

Makes: 2

Preparation Time: 8mins

Ingredient List:

- 1 pint coconut ice cream
- 6-8 samoas cookies (any brand, chopped)
- ⅓ cup whole milk
- 2 ounces coconut rum

Toppings:

- Whipped cream
- Caramel sauce

Instructions:

1. In a food blender, add the ice cream, along with the cookies, milk, and rum and blend on moderate speed until silky smooth.

2. Pour the shake into Collins glasses and top with whipped cream and caramel sauce.

Recipe 40: Coco Loco Key Lime Pie

Milkshake

A boozy milkshake that is a dreamy, creamy combination of key lime and coconut cream pie.

Makes: 2-3

Preparation Time: 5mins

Ingredient List:

- ¼ Cup Irish Cream liqueur
- 3 cups vanilla bean ice cream
- 3 tablespoons lime flavor vodka
- 3 tablespoons freshly squeezed key lime juice

- 3 tablespoons coconut rum
- 2 tablespoons tequila
- 1 pound graham crackers (approximately)*

Toppings:

- Whip cream
- Freshly grated lime zest
- Shredded coconut (toasted_

Instructions:

1. Add the liqueur, ice cream, vodka, lime juice, rum, tequila, and crackers in a food blender and process until silky smooth.

2. Pour the shake into four glasses, top with whip cream, and garnish with lime zest and shredded coconut.

* The number of crackers will depend on your desired consistency.

Dark Chocolate Cardamom Shake

Dark Chocolate Cardamom Shake is a decadent drink with a classic and nostalgic taste. Also, it is a modern and gregarious drink with some amazing ingredients like vanilla bean ice cream, black cardamom, cocoa powder, sugar and milk.

Serving Size: 1

Cooking Time: 10 minutes

Ingredients:

- 4 scoops vanilla bean ice cream
- 1 tsp black cardamom
- 1/3 cup milk
- 3 tbsp dark cocoa powder
- 1 tsp sugar

Instructions:

1. Combine all the ingredients in the blender.

2. Blend until smooth.

3. Dark chocolate cardamom shake is ready to serve.

Hot Fudge Bourbon Milkshake

Hot Fudge Bourbon Milkshake is a crunchy, sweet, delicious shake to offer your kids. Special childhood treats for your loved ones with vanilla ice cream, bourbon, hot fudge, and vanilla essence. It's a special taste with the twist of fudge that looks amazing.

Serving Size: 2

Cooking Time: 5 Minutes

Ingredients:

- 1.5 cups vanilla ice cream
- 1 tsp vanilla essence
- 2 oz burbon
- 1/2 cup hot fudge

For burbon whip cream

- 1 tbsp heavy cream
- 1 tbsp burbon
- 1 tbsp sugar

Instructions:

1. In the blender, combine ice cream, sugar, vanilla essence, burbon and ¼ cup of hot fudge. Blend until smooth.

2. Add hot fudge in the bottom of the glass.

3. Pour into glasses. Garnish with burbon and whipped cream and hot fudge.

4. Hot fudge burbon milkshake is ready to serve.

Cookies n Cream Milkshake

Cookies n Cream Milkshake has a creamy, chocolatey, and crunchy texture and flavor. It's a simple to make and quick milkshake recipe. Crush cookies and enjoy the chilled taste. It's a smooth, delicious, and only 3-ingredient recipe.

Serving Size: 2

Cooking Time: 5 Minutes

Ingredients:

- 5 chocolate sandwich cookies
- 2 cups vanilla ice cream
- 1/4 cup milk

Instructions:

1. Place cookies in zip lock bag. Crush cookies.

2. Now in blender, combine milk, & vanilla ice cream. Blend until smooth.

3. Add crushed cookies and blend again.

4. Pour in glasses. Garnish with cookies.

5. Cookies n cream milkshake is ready.

Peach Milkshake

Peach milkshake is a tangy, sweet and refreshing milkshake recipe. It's an only-4-ingredient recipe with smooth texture and flavor. The orange color makes it look cooler and expressive milkshake. Enjoy making it at home for your loved ones. Also, you can use frozen peaches to make this shake.

Serving Size: 2

Cooking Time: 5 minutes

Ingredients:

- 2 cups fresh peach
- ¾ cup milk
- 1.5 cups vanilla ice cream
- 1 tsp sugar

Instructions:

1. Add peach pieces into blender. Blend until turns into smooth puree.

2. Then add sugar, milk, and vanilla ice cream.

3. Blend until smooth and amazing texture.

4. Peach milkshake is ready to serve.

Pumpkin Milkshake

Pumpkin Milkshake is a cozy, cool, and creamy treat for your loved ones and family. It's healthy and taste best with frozen yogurt, pumpkin, and spices. You can choose multiple toppings like graham crackers, whipped cream, chocolate sauce, and caramel sauce. It certainly takes less than 5 minutes to prepare the perfect shake for the fall.

Serving Size: 2

Cooking Time: 5 Minutes

Ingredients:

- ½ cup pumpkin puree
- ¼ cup milk
- ½ medium banana
- ½ cup frozen yogurt
- ¼ tsp ground cinnamon

- Whipped cream, for garnishing
- 1 tsp pumpkin pie spices
- 1 full sheet graham cracker

Instructions:

1. In the blender, pumpkin puree, milk, banana, yogurt, pumpkin spice pie, and cinnamon.

2. Break the cookies into crumbs in a zip bag and pressing them with a rolling pin. Then add to blender. Blend until smooth.

3. Divide into glasses and topped with whipped cream, and cracker cookies.

4. Pumpkin milkshake is ready.

Salted Caramel Milkshake

Salted Caramel Milkshake is made with vanilla caramel sauce, dark chocolate, and bean ice cream. It's a delicious creamy milkshake with extra caramel feeling. A simple to make, salty milkshake.

Serving Size: 2

Cooking Time: 5 Minutes

Ingredients:

- ¼ cup salted caramel sauce
- ½ cup milk
- ½ cup whipped cream
- 4 cups vanilla ice cream

Instructions:

1. Add milk, salted caramel sauce, and ice cream in the blender. Then, blend until smooth.

2. Add whipped cream. Transfer to the tall glasses.

3. Garnish with dark chocolate and salted caramel sauce.

4. Salted caramel milkshake is ready.

Cherry Vanilla Milkshake

Cherry Vanilla Milkshake is simple and delicious with a crazy cherry flavor. Just made with simple ingredients like milk, vanilla ice cream, and cherries. It's yummy, tummy-filling, healthy, and refreshing. Start your morning with this milkshake.

Serving Size: 2

Cooking Time: 15 Minutes

Ingredients:

- ¼ cup milk
- 3 scoops vanilla ice cream
- 1 cup cherries

Instructions:

1. Place all the ingredients in the blender. Blend until smooth.

2. Cherry vanilla milkshake is ready to serve.

Mint White Chocolate Milkshake

Mint White Chocolate Milkshake is rich, thick, and refreshing. It's the best combination of mint and chocolate. Cool your jets in a hot afternoon with this special recipe. All mint lovers are going to love this combination.

Serving Size: 2

Cooking Time: 5 minutes

Ingredients:

- 3 cups white mint chocolate ice cream
- 1.5 cups milk
- Whipped cream, as needed

Instructions:

1. Place milk and white mint chocolate ice cream in the blender.

2. Blend until smooth. Pour in the glass.

3. Garnish with whipped cream. Mint white chocolate milkshake is ready.

Peanut Butter Brownie Milkshake

Peanut Butter Brownie Milkshake is frosty, thick, and frothy. The blend of peanut butter, brownie, and ice cream tastes amazing. You can garnish it with whipped cream, some brownie bites and also chocolate syrup to give it extra flavor at the beginning.

Serving Size: 2

Cooking Time: 5 minutes

Ingredients:

- ¾ cup brownie, crumbled
- ¼ cup peanut butter
- 6 scoops vanilla ice cream
- ¾ cup milk

Instructions:

1. Put brownie, milk, peanut butter and vanilla ice cream in the blender. Blend until smooth.

2. Serve in the tall glasses and top up with some brownies and straw.

3. Peanut butter brownie milkshake is ready.

Oreo Milkshake

Oreo Milkshake is a super cool and easy recipe made with milk, Oreo cookies, and vanilla ice cream. The sweet treat for your family and kids in the hot summer to enjoy at home. It's delicious, chocolatey, and full of flavors of Oreo. Garnish it with some Oreo cookies and whipped cream to make it look fanatic.

Serving Size: 2

Cooking Time: 5 minutes

Ingredients:

- 2/3 cup milk
- 2 cups vanilla ice cream
- 8 Oreo cookies
- 1 tsp vanilla essence
- Whipped cream, as needed

Instructions:

1. Add milk, vanilla essence, ice cream, and Oreo cookies in the blender. Blend until smooth.

2. Serve in the large glass and garnish with whipped cream and Oreo cookies.

3. Oreo milkshake is ready.

Strawberry Milkshake

Strawberry Milkshake is a classic, rich, and creamy texture drink. You can make it with fresh or frozen strawberries. It's actually easy to make with just a few ingredients like milk, strawberries, vanilla ice cream, and sugar. A perfect summery fruity treat for your kids at home.

Serving Size: 2

Cooking Time: 5 minutes

Ingredients:

- 3 cups strawberries
- 2 tbsp sugar

- 1 tsp vanilla essence
- ½ cup milk

Instructions:

1. Combined sliced strawberries, vanilla essence, sugar in a mixing bowl. Stir well and macerate for 20 minutes.

2. In the mixer, add strawberries, milk, and vanilla ice cream. Blend until smooth. Pour in the glasses garnish with strawberries chunks on the top.

3. Strawberry milkshake is ready to serve.

Banana Milkshake

Banana Milkshake is a delicious, tummy-filling and mouthwatering drink. You can enjoy this classic simple recipe at home during breakfast or even snack time. This one is healthy and special to include in your diet as well. To make it more luscious, you can add dates, cinnamon, and almonds.

Serving Size: 6

Cooking Time: 6 minutes

Ingredients:

- 2 bananas
- 4 dates
- ½ tsp cinnamon
- 2 ice cubes
- 1.5 cups chilled milk
- 6 almonds, soaked

Instructions:

1. Add almonds, dates, and sugar in the blender. Then put cinnamon and cardamom powder. Pour milk and water.

2. Blend in the mixer.

3. Now add banana and ice cubes. Blend again until frothy and smooth.

4. Banana milkshake is ready to serve.

Chocolate Chip Cookie Milkshake

Chocolate Chip Cookie Milkshake is a perfect afterschool milkshake. It's tasty, delicious with cream, milk, and chocolate. It's the perfect combination of silky vanilla ice cream with rich and chocolaty flavor. A heavenly combination with a crunch of chocolate chips.

Serving Size: 2

Cooking Time: 20 minutes

Ingredients:

- 1 cup milk

- 2 cups vanilla ice cream
- 3 chocolate chip cookies, crushed
- Whipped cream, for garnishing

Instructions:

1. Place vanilla ice cream, chocolate chip cookies, milk, and whip cream in the blender.

2. Blend until soft. Make sure it's smooth enough.

3. Pour in the tall glass and garnish with whipped cream.

4. Chocolate chip cookies milkshake is ready to serve.

Date Milkshake

Date Milkshake is healthy, creamy, and full of nutrition. Also, it's great for tummy-filling experience and kids will love it. A unique beverage with nutrition and taste. Sweet dates and vanilla flavored milk are blended to make a blasting shake.

Serving Size: 2

Cooking Time: 5 minutes

Ingredients:

- 3 cups milk
- 10 dates
- ¼ tsp cinnamon powder

Instructions:

1. In the blender, blend dates chunks without seed.

2. Then add chilled milk, and cinnamon powder.

3. Blend well until smooth. Then add ice cream and some ice for the texture blend again.

4. Date milkshake is ready.

Blueberry Milkshake

Blueberry Milkshake is a cool and refreshing drink to dazzle your day. A perfect morning milkshake to boost your mood with some fresh or frozen blueberries. It's made from natural berries and gives fresh flavors. The minimal ingredients make it a perfect blend for everyone.

Serving Size: 4

Cooking Time: 10 minutes

Ingredients:

- 2 cups frozen blueberries

- 2 cups milk
- 2 cups vanilla ice cream
- 2 tbsp honey
- Whipped cream, for garnishing

Instructions:

1. In a blender, add frozen berries, vanilla ice cream, honey and blend it well until smooth puree.

2. Pour in the jar and garnish with whipped cream and top up with a blueberry.

3. Blueberry milkshake is ready to serve.

Butterscotch Milkshake

Butterscotch Milkshake is a soft, buttery, creamy, and frothy treat. It is the mixer of butterscotch ice cream, butterscotch sauce, and chips. It's crunchy and tasty. The butterscotch is an all-time cool summer treat for kids and elders in the house. Easy to make and get ready quickly. Add more ice to make it a chill drink.

Serving Size: 2

Cooking Time: 10 minutes

Ingredients:

- 1 scoop butterscotch ice cream
- 1 cup milk
- 2 tsp butterscotch sauce

- 3 ice cubes
- 2 tsp butterscotch chips

Instructions:

1. Place milk, and ice cubes in the blender.

2. Then add butterscotch ice cream, sauce and chips. Blend until frothy.

3. In the serving glass, slide in butterscotch sauce with spoon. Pour the mixer.

4. Butterscotch milkshake is ready to serve.

Nutella Milkshake

Nutella Milkshake is a creamy, chocolaty and decadent drink. It's a perfect homemade recipe to treat your time with the best flavor. Amazing milkshake recipe with few ingredients. Nutella is the best milkshake flavor for every age group.

Serving Size: 2

Cooking Time: 5 minutes

Ingredients:

- 1 cup milk
- 1/3 cup Nutella
- 3 scoops vanilla

Instructions:

1. Add milk, Nutella and vanilla in the blender. Blend it until smooth.

2. Pour in the glass. Nutella milkshake is ready.

KitKat Milkshake

KitKat Milkshake is a simple, classic, and crunchy shake. The delicious shake you can prepare with milk, vanilla ice cream, and some chocolate syrup as well. A new taste for those who are fond of new flavors. During summer vacations, kids are going to enjoy this treat at home.

Serving Size: 2

Cooking Time: 10 minutes

Ingredients:

- 2 KitKat bars
- 2 cups vanilla ice cream
- 1 tsp vanilla essence
- ½ cup milk
- Chocolate syrup, for garnishing
- Whipped cream, for garnishing

Instructions:

1. Combine ice cream, milk, KitKat bar, syrup and vanilla essence in the blender. Blend until smooth.

2. Pour in the glass and top with whipped cream.

3. Kit Kat milkshake is ready to serve.

Chocolate Cashew Milkshake

Chocolate Cashew Milkshake is rich, creamy, chocolaty, and quick to make. Also, it's thick and looks luxurious. It's loaded with classy ingredients and makes your milkshake the perfect one.

Serving Size: 1

Cooking Time: 5 minutes

Ingredients:

- 1 cup milk
- 3 tsp cocoa powder
- 3 tbsp cashew
- 1 pinch salt
- 1 banana, ripped

Instructions:

1. Place milk, banana, cocoa powder, salt, milk, and cashew in the blender. Blend until smooth.

2. Pour in the glass. Chocolate cashew milkshake is ready to serve.

Mango Yogurt Milkshake

Mango Yogurt Milkshake is tangy, flavorful, and delicious. It is super smooth mixed with crushed ice, mango, honey, lime juice, and a dash of cinnamon. One can also add Greek yogurt for all health purposes. In summer, a chilled glass of mango yogurt milkshake is just perfect.

Serving Size: 1

Cooking Time: 5 minutes

Ingredients:

- 2 cups frozen mango chunks
- ¼ tsp ground cinnamon
- ½ tbsp honey

- 1 tsp lime juice
- 1 cup yogurt

Instructions:

1. Place yogurt, mango chunks, lime juice, cinnamon, and honey. Blend until smooth and frothy.

2. Pour in the glass. Mango yogurt milkshake is ready to serve.

Pineapple Coconut Milkshake

Pineapple Coconut Milkshake is fresh, tangy, and fruity. It's simple to make and energizes your mood and body. It's healthy and full of protein. You can even enjoy this during the summer season to hydrate your body.

Serving Size: 1

Cooking Time: 5 minutes

Ingredients:

- 1 cup frozen pineapple, chunks
- ¼ cup yogurt
- ¼ cup coconut milk
- ¼ cup milk
- ½ tbsp coconut
- Ice, handful

Instructions:

1. Put ice, coconut milk, pineapple chunks, yogurt, and regular milk in the blender.

2. Blend until smooth. Pour in the glass and top up with some pineapple chunks & shredded coconut.

3. Pineapple coconut milkshake is ready.

Apple Pie Milkshake

Apple Pie Milkshake is a classic, rich, and sweet treat. It can be served as a dessert. It is made with leftover apple pie, milk, corn starch, cinnamon, salt, water, and vanilla ice cream.

Serving Size: 6

Cooking Time: 25 minutes

Ingredients:

- ¼ cup brown sugar
- 1 tbsp corn starch
- ½ tsp cinnamon
- ¾ cup water
- 1 tbsp milk
- 1 cup vanilla ice cream

Instructions:

1. In the saucepan, combine apple, brown sugar, cornstarch, cinnamon, water, and salt. Cook on medium heat until apple softens. Let it cool aside.

2. Add in blender and puree it. Then place ice cream in it. Then add apple pie as well and milk. Blend until smooth.

3. Pour in the glass. Top up with some caramel sauce on it.

4. Apple pie milkshake is ready to serve.

Coffee Caramel Milkshake

Coffee Caramel Milkshake is a thick, smooth, and complete package of three special ingredients: vanilla ice cream, caramel sauce, and coffee. A perfect combination milkshake to offer your guest at home. It's easy to make a coffee concentrated milkshake.

Serving Size: 2

Cooking Time: 10 minutes

Ingredients:

- ¼ cup caramel sauce
- 2 cups milk
- 10 ice cubes
- 2 tsp sugar
- 1.5 tsp ground coffee

Instructions:

1. Place caramel syrup, milk, ground coffee, ice cubes, and sugar. Blend well until smooth.

2. Pour in the serving glass and topped up with whipped cream.

3. Drizzle some caramel syrup. Coffee caramel milkshake is ready.

Red Velvet Cheesecake Milkshake

Red Velvet Cheesecake Milkshake is a delicious way to celebrate love or date night. It's made with cake mix and ice cream that is the perfect indulgent for a romantic date. The color and the texture are so pretty amazing that it gives you a perfect feeling inside your mouth.

Serving Size: 1

Cooking Time: 5 minutes

Ingredients:

- 1 red velvet cake
- ½ cup milk
- 2 scoops vanilla ice cream

Instructions:

1. In the blender, add milk and vanilla ice cream. The break red velvet cake inside. Stir into milkshake and blend well.

2. Serve in the glass. Red velvet cheesecake milkshake is ready.

Almond Saffron Milkshake

Almond Saffron Milkshake is a healthy and refreshing drink. It's a crunchy and nutritious breakfast dessert. Before making it, soak almonds for 20 minutes. Also, it's a creamy nutty-flavored shake. Garnish with saffron for a rich feeling.

Serving Size: 2

Cooking Time: 15 minutes

Ingredients:

- 1 tbsp walnut
- 1 tsp flax seed
- 2 tbsp almonds
- 1 tsp honey
- 2-3 saffron
- 1 cup milk

Instructions:

1. Firstly, put almond and walnut in the blender. Grind it.

2. Then add honey, milk, flax seeds, cold milk and saffron. Blend well.

3. Pour in the glass. Almond saffron milkshake is ready to serve.

Beetroot Milkshake

Beetroot Milkshake is healthy, nutritious, and delicious for kids. It's an excellent shake for breakfast to start your day. A wonderful and chilled milkshake to enjoy on hot summer days. This is also healthy for kids. Moreover, it's very healthy to enjoy with family. To add more color and liveliness to the shake, you can use the rose syrup as well.

Serving Size: 2

Cooking Time: 10 minutes

Ingredients:

- 2 beetroots, pilled and boiled
- 4 oz milk
- 2 scoops vanilla ice cream
- 1 tsp cinnamon powder
- Crushed ice, handful

Instructions:

1. Firstly, make the beetroot puree in the blender.

2. Then add ice cream, sugar syrup, cinnamon powder, crushed ice and milk. Blend until smooth.

3. Pour in the glass. Beetroot milkshake is ready to serve.

Pistachio Milkshake

Pistachio Milkshake is a royal, crunchy, and smooth drink. You can make it using milk, sugar, chopped pistachio, and cardamom powder. You can also add pistachio or vanilla ice cream for a silky texture. Serve it immediately for its cold, nutty, sweet flavor.

Serving Size: 2

Cooking Time: 5 minutes

Ingredients:

- 1 cup milk
- 3-4 scoops vanilla ice cream
- 1 tsp chopped pistachio + 1 tsp for garnishing
- A pinch of cardamom powder
- 1 tsp sugar

Instructions:

112

1. In the blender, add milk, chopped pistachio, sugar, and cardamom powder.

2. Add ice cream scoops. Blend it until smooth.

3. Serve it in the tall glasses. Pistachio milkshake is ready.

Orange Milkshake

Orange Milkshake is a zesty, nutrition-rich, and creamy milkshake. It is made with orange, vanilla ice cream, and almond milk. Also, it's a protein-rich shake full of almond and orange flavors. Moreover, it has vitamin C, which is good for the immune system.

Serving Size: 1

Cooking Time: 10 minutes

Ingredients:

- 1 orange
- ¼ cup vanilla ice cream
- ¼ cup almond milk

Instructions:

1. Cut oranges in halves. In the blender, put oranges, vanilla ice cream and almond milk.

2. Blend until smooth and creamy.

3. Pour in the glass. Orange milkshake is ready.

Custard Apple Milkshake

Custard Apple Milkshake is a sweet, dessert-like, and lovely flavor drink. Scoop flesh from the custard apple and mix with other ingredients like milk, sugar, or honey. It's an exotic flavor milkshake with a thick consistency.

Serving Size: 2

Cooking Time: 20 minutes

Ingredients:

- 3 custard apples, ripped
- 1.5 cups milk
- 2-3 tsp sugar

Instructions:

1. Scoop the pulp out of custard apple and put in blender. Remember to put out the seeds.

2. Then add sugar and blend again.

3. Now add milk to thicken the shake.

4. Serve it in the glass. Custard apple milkshake is ready.

Sapota & Nut Milkshake

Sapota & Nut Milkshake is a protein booster with smashing ingredients. Also, it's an energy drink for kids as it contains milk, sapota, cashew nuts, and walnuts. Moreover, sapota provides carbohydrates to brain cells and good for mental health.

Serving Size: 5

Cooking Time: 10 minutes

Ingredients:

- 2 cups sapota cubes
- 3 cups milk
- 2 tbsp chopped cashew nuts
- 2 tbsp sugar
- 2 tbsp chopped walnut

Instructions:

1. Add milk, sapota, cashew nuts, and sugar in the blender. Blend until smooth.

2. Pour milkshake into glasses. Garnish with chopped walnut.

3. Sapota & Nut milkshake is ready to serve.

Black Current Milkshake

Black Current Milkshake is a creamy and yummy drink for summer. It's pretty easy to make and has tangy flavors. You can enjoy this as breakfast as well. It's made with simple ingredients like milk, black current ice cream, and sugar.

Serving Size: 1

Cooking Time: 10 minutes

Ingredients:

- 1 cup milk
- 3 scoops black current ice cream
- Sugar, as per taste

Instructions:

1. In the blender, combine milk, black current ice cream and sugar.

2. Blend until smooth.

3. Pour milkshake into glasses.

4. Black current milkshake is ready.

Kiwi Milkshake

Kiwi Milkshake is thick and creamy. It is the perfect drink for summer. Also, it's sour but sweet. Made with fresh kiwis, milk and sugar. It's a wonderful shake with only 3 ingredients.

Serving Size: 1

Cooking Time: 5 minutes

Ingredients:

- 2 kiwifruits, peeled
- ½ cup milk
- 1 tsp sugar

Instructions:

1. In the blender, combine milk, kiwi and sugar.

2. Blend until smooth texture.

3. Serve in the glass. Kiwi milkshake is ready.

Lemon Flavored Milkshake

Lemon Flavored Milkshake is bursting with zesty flavors, thick and creamy. No wonder it turns out to be the best shake. Also, it's sweet enough for kids. A delicious take on with no guilt. Made with fresh lemons, coconut milk, vanilla yogurt, and maple syrup. It's amazing refreshing shake with only 4 ingredients.

Serving Size: 2

Cooking Time: 10 minutes

Ingredients:

- ½ cup lemon juice
- 2 tbsp vanilla yogurt

- 13.5 oz coconut milk
- ¼ cup maple syrup

Instructions:

1. Add lemon juice and half can of coconut milk to ice trays and freeze it for 4 hours.

2. Add another half can of coconut milk, lemon juice, vanilla yogurt and maple syrup in the blender until it becomes smooth.

3. Add ice cubes in the shake.

4. Serve in the glass. Lemon flavored milkshake is ready.

Avocado Milkshake

Avocado Milkshake is a healthy shake made with only 3 ingredients. It's delicious and also best for breakfast. Also, it's an incredibly fantastic shake that will make you feel heavy and also boost your morning mood. Made with avocado, milk, and sugar or honey.

Serving Size: 2

Cooking Time: 5 minutes

Ingredients:

- 1 ripe avocado
- 2 cups milk
- 3 tbsp sugar or honey

Instructions:

1. Scoop the pulp out of avocado with spoon and put in blender. Then add sugar and milk.

2. Blend until smooth. Pour in the glass.

3. Avocado milkshake is ready to serve.

Carrot Milkshake

Carrot Milkshake is a healthy and easy to make shake. It's nutritious and healthy for kids and elders. It is a very unique approach and helps you beat the summer heat. Moreover, your eyes are protected with carrot, and it is also called as a superfood.

Serving Size: 1

Cooking Time: 5 minutes

Ingredients:

- ½ cup grated carrot
- 4-5 almonds
- 4 dates
- 1 ¼ cups milk

Instructions:

1. Soak almonds in water for 30 minutes. Now heat the pan and add grated carrot and sauté them on low heat. Add little bit of water.

2. Do not overcook.

3. Put in the blender and milk.

4. Then add soaked almonds & dates. Blend until smooth.

5. Carrot milkshake is ready to serve.

Rice Krispie Milkshake

Rice Krispie Milkshake is a delicious treat to surprise your kids. It's a fun and delicious milkshake. Made with all the classic flavors like vanilla bean ice cream, marshmallow, milk and rice krispe treat.

Serving Size: 2-3

Cooking Time: 15 minutes

Ingredients:

- 1 3/4 cups vanilla ice cream
- 1/2 cup milk
- 1/2 marshmallow fluff
- 1/2 cup rice krispies
- Ice cubes, handful

Instructions:

1. Combine Vanilla bean nice cream milk and marshmallow fluff in the blender blend until become smooth.

2. Add in krispie cereal and again blend it.

3. Now garnish with a whip cream marshmallow and more krispie cereal.

4. Rice krispie milkshake is ready to serve.

Cinnamon Milkshake

Cinnamon milkshake is a yummy and interesting beverage. It is made with cinnamon powder and milk, and it's a very easy to make recipe. Enjoy this powerful shake at home with your family members for the perfect healthy solution. Every sip of it is thick and creamy and tastes just unique.

Serving Size: 2

Cooking Time: 10 minutes

Ingredients:

- 1/2 tbsp vanilla essence
- 1 cup cold milk
- 1/4 tbsp cinnamon powder
- Nutmeg powder, to taste
- 2 cups vanilla ice cream

Instructions:

1. In the blender combine vanilla essence cold milk, cinnamon powder, nutmeg powder and vanilla ice cream.

2. Blend well until smooth.

3. Power in the shake glass and cinnamon milkshake is ready to serve.

Sweet Cherry Vanilla Milkshake

Sweet cherry-vanilla milkshake is a simple and delicious recipe. It's just made with vanilla ice cream, milk and some sweet cherries. Moreover, it's truly a special drink for the summer season. You will enjoy the color contrast that it creates.

Serving Size: 2

Cooking Time: 15 minutes

Ingredients:

- 1/4 cup milk
- 3 scoops vanilla ice cream
- 1 cup cherries, frozen

Instructions:

1. In the blender combine milk vanilla ice cream and cherries. Blend until smooth.

2. Pour in the glass.

3. Sweet cherry vanilla milkshake is ready to serve.

Raspberry Milkshake

Raspberry milkshake is a creamy delicious and easy recipe with the frozen raspberries and some whipped cream. It's only a three-ingredient recipe combining ice cream, milk and raspberry.

Serving Size: 2

Cooking Time: 5 minutes

Ingredients:

- 6 oz frozen raspberries
- 1/2 cup milk
- 2 scoops raspberry frozen yogurt

Instructions:

1. In the blender combine frozen raspberries with milk and frozen yogurt and whisk until smooth.

2. Pour in the glass. Raspberry milkshake is ready to serve.

Pina Colada Vanilla Milkshake

Pina colada milkshake is a sweet, refreshing, and boozy drink that is made of vanilla ice cream, pineapple juice, pineapple chunks, coconut milk, and some rum. It's a fun treat for your friends and loved ones. Have a conversation with your buddies over Pina colada shake and enjoy your time.

Serving Size: 2

Cooking Time: 15 minutes

Ingredients:

For rim the glass

- 1/4 cup honey
- 1 /2 cup toasted coconut

For Pina Colada milkshake

- 4 cups vanilla ice cream
- 1/3 cup pineapple chunks
- 1/4 cup pineapple juice
- 1/4 cup coconut milk
- 1/4 cup Rum

Instructions:

1. Ring the milkshake glasses with a honey and toasted coconut. Please glasses in the freezer.

2. Combine vanilla ice cream pineapple chunks pineapple juice coconut milk and drum into the blender. Blend until smooth and creamy.

3. Pour into the glasses. Pina colada milkshake is ready to serve.

Banana Almond and Oat Milkshake

Preparation Time: **5 minutes**

Yield: 2 servings

Ingredients

1 large (180 g) frozen banana, cut into small pieces

1 scoop (60 g) vanilla ice cream

1 tablespoon (7 g) rolled oats

1 ½ cups (375 ml) almond milk, unsweetened

Banana slices, for garnish

Method
1. Combine the banana, vanilla ice cream, rolled oats, and almond milk in a blender. Process until it becomes smooth.
2. Pour mixture into 2 serving glasses. Garnish with banana slices.
3. Enjoy!

Nutritional Information:

Energy – 291 kcal, Fat - 10.2 g, Carbs - 47.4 g, Protein - 5.3 g, Sodium - 205 mg

Blackberry Banana Milkshake with Flax

Preparation Time: **5 minutes**

Yield: 2 servings

Ingredients

1 cup (150 g) frozen blackberries, plus more for garnish

1 large (180 g) frozen banana, cut into small pieces

1 scoop (60 g) vanilla flavored ice cream

1 cup (250 ml) skim milk

1 tablespoon (10 g) flaxseeds

Fresh mint sprigs

Method

1. Combine the blackberries, banana, vanilla ice cream, milk, and flaxseeds in a blender. Process until it becomes smooth.
2. Pour mixture into 2 serving glasses. Garnish with some blackberries and fresh mint sprigs.
3. Enjoy!

Nutritional Information:

Energy - 210 kcal, Fat - 7.2 g, Carbs - 31.0 g, Protein - 7.2 g, Sodium - 73 mg

Chocolate Banana and Soy Milkshake

Preparation Time: **5 minutes**

Yield: 2 servings

Ingredients

1 large (180 g) frozen banana, cut into small pieces

1 scoop (60 g) chocolate ice cream

1 cup (250 ml) soy milk, unsweetened

4 ice cubes

Dark chocolate shavings, to serve

137

Method

1. Combine the banana, chocolate ice cream, soy milk, and ice cubes in a blender. Process until it becomes smooth.
2. Pour mixture into 2 serving glasses. Garnish with some chocolate shavings.
3. Enjoy!

Nutritional Information:

Energy - 228 kcal, Fat - 6.9 g, Carbs - 35.1 g, Protein - 7.9 g, Sodium - 121 mg

Pink Raspberry Almond Milkshake

Preparation Time: **5 minutes**

Yield: 2 servings

Ingredients

1 cup (250 g) frozen raspberries, plus more for garnish

1 cup (250 g) almond milk

1 scoop (60 g) vanilla ice cream

1 tablespoon (15 ml) peppermint syrup

Fresh mint sprigs

Method

1. Combine the raspberries, almond milk, vanilla ice cream, and peppermint syrup in a blender. Process until smooth and creamy.
2. Transfer mixture into 2 chilled glasses. Garnish with raspberries and mint sprigs.
3. Enjoy!

Nutritional Information:

Energy - 227 kcal, Fat - 5 g, Carbs - 44.7 g, Protein - 2.5 g, Sodium - 103 mg

Cherry Banana and Vanilla Milkshake

Preparation Time: **5 minutes**

Yield: 2 servings

Ingredients

1 cup (150 g) pitted cherries, plus more for garnish

1 large (180 g) frozen banana, cut into small pieces

2 scoops (120 g) vanilla ice cream

1 cup (250 ml) whole milk

Fresh mint sprigs

Method

1. Combine the cherries, banana, vanilla ice cream, and milk in a blender. Process until it becomes smooth.
2. Pour mixture into 2 chilled glasses. Garnish with some cherries and mint sprigs.
3. Enjoy!

Nutritional Information:

Energy - 273 kcal, Fat - 7.3 g, Carbs - 44.7 g, Protein - 7.8 g, Sodium - 119 mg

Banana and Date Milkshake

Preparation Time: **5 minutes**

Yield: 2 servings

Ingredients

1 large (180 g) frozen banana, cut into small pieces

3 (10 g) dates, pitted

2 scoops (120 g) vanilla ice cream

1 ½ cups (375 ml) skim milk

Banana slices, for garnish

Method

1. Combine the banana, dates, vanilla ice cream, and milk in a blender. Process until smooth and creamy.
2. Pour mixture into 2 chilled glasses. Garnish with a slice of banana.
3. Enjoy!

Nutritional Information:

Energy - 226 kcal, Fat - 3.6 g, Carbs - 40.5 g, Protein - 8.3 g, Sodium - 124 mg

Spiced Mango Yogurt Milkshake

Preparation Time: **5 minutes**

Yield: 2 servings

Ingredients

1 cup (165 g) diced mangoes

2 scoops (120 g) vanilla ice cream

1/2 cup (125 g) Greek yogurt

1/2 cup (125 ml) low-fat milk

1/2 teaspoon (2.5 g) ginger (grated)

6 ice cubes

Fresh mint sprig

Method

1. Combine the mango, ice cream, yogurt, milk, ginger, and ice cubes in a high-speed blender. Process until smooth and creamy.

2. Pour into 2 chilled glasses. Garnish with mint sprigs.
3. Serve and enjoy!

Nutritional Information:

Energy - 234 kcal, Fat - 5.8 g, Carbs - 38.4 g, Protein - 9.7 g, Sodium - 75 mg

Chocolate Hazelnut Milkshake

Preparation Time: **5 minutes**

Yield: 2 servings

Ingredients

2 scoops (120 g) chocolate flavored ice cream

1 cup (250 ml) skim milk

2 tablespoons (30 ml) hazelnut syrup

6 ice cubes

Whipped cream

Chocolate shavings

Method

1. Combine the ice cream, milk, hazelnut syrup, and ice cubes in a blender. Process until it becomes smooth.
2. Pour mixture into 2 chilled glasses. Add some whipped cream and chocolate shavings on top.
3. Enjoy!

Nutritional Information:

Energy - 217 kcal, Fat - 10.1 g, Carbs - 25.4 g, Protein - 7.2 g, Sodium - 115 mg

Banana Apricot and Oat Milkshake

Preparation Time: **5 minutes**

Yield: 2 servings

Ingredients

1 large (180 g) frozen banana, cut into small pieces

2 scoops (120 g) vanilla ice cream

1 cup (250 ml) whole milk

1/2 cup (85 g) apricots, diced

2 tablespoons (15 g) rolled oats, plus more for garnish

Fresh mint sprigs

Method

1. Combine the banana, ice cream, milk, apricots, oats, and ice cubes in a high-speed blender. Process until smooth and creamy.
2. Pour into 2 chilled glasses. Garnish with some oats and mint sprigs.
3. Serve and enjoy.

Nutritional Information:

Energy - 210 kcal, Fat - 4.1 g, Carbs - 37.4 g,
Protein - 6.8 g, Sodium - 93 mg

Creamy Strawberry Banana Milkshake

Preparation Time: **5 minutes**

Yield: 2 servings

Ingredients

1 cup (220 g) frozen strawberries, hulled

1 large (180 g) frozen banana, cut into small pieces

2 scoops (120 g) vanilla ice cream

1 cup (250 ml) skim milk

Fresh mint sprigs

Method

1. Combine the frozen strawberries, banana, vanilla ice cream, and milk in a blender. Process until it becomes smooth.
2. Pour mixture into 2 chilled glasses. Garnish with some strawberries and mint sprigs.
3. Enjoy.

Nutritional Information:

Energy - 213 kcal, Fat - 3.7 g, Carbs - 37.0 g, Protein - 7.8 g, Sodium - 125 mg

Chocolate Milkshake with Cinnamon

Preparation Time: **5 minutes**

Yield: 2 servings

Ingredients

2 scoops (120 g) chocolate flavored ice cream

1 ½ cups (375 ml) almond milk

2 tablespoons (30 ml) chocolate syrup

1/4 teaspoon (0.5 g) cinnamon, ground

6 ice cubes

Whipped cream, to serve

Chocolate shavings, to serve

Method

1. Combine the ice cream, milk, chocolate syrup, cinnamon, and ice cubes in a blender. Process until it becomes smooth.
2. Pour mixture into 2 chilled glasses. Add a spoonful of whipped cream and chocolate shavings on top.
3. Serve and enjoy.

Nutritional Information:

Energy - 235 kcal, Fat - 7.2 g, Carbs - 34.4 g, Protein - 6.7 g, Sodium - 132 mg

Peach Ginger and Almond Milkshake

Preparation Time: 5 minutes

Yield: 2 servings

Ingredients

1 large (175 g) peach, peeled, stoned, and cut into small pieces

1/2 teaspoon (2.5 g) ginger, grated

1 cup (250 ml) almond milk

1 cup (250 g) frozen yogurt

6 ice cubes

Fresh mint sprigs

Method

1. Combine the peach, ginger, almond milk, yogurt, and ice cubes in your blender. Process until smooth and creamy.

2. Pour milkshake into 2 chilled glasses. Garnish with mint sprigs.
3. Serve and enjoy.

Nutritional Information:

Energy - 163 kcal, Fat - 3.2 g, Carbs - 23.4 g, Protein - 8.9 g, Sodium - 161 mg

-

Blueberry Banana Soy Milkshake

Preparation Time: **5 minutes**

Yield: 2 servings

Ingredients

1 cup (155 g) frozen blueberries, plus more for garnish

1 large (180 g) frozen banana, cut into small pieces

1 scoop (60 g) vanilla ice cream

1 ½ cups (375 ml) soy milk

Fresh mint sprigs

Method

1. Place the blueberries, banana, ice cream, and soy milk in a high-speed blender. Process until smooth and creamy.
2. Pour into 2 chilled glasses. Garnish with some blueberries and mint sprigs.
3. Serve and enjoy!

Nutritional Information:

Energy - 230 kcal, Fat - 3.9 g, Carbs - 41.0 g, Protein - 8.3 g, Sodium - 125 mg

Watermelon Plum and Kiwi Milkshake

Preparation Time: **5 minutes**

Yield: 2 servings

Ingredients

1 cup (150 g) watermelon, diced

1/2 cup (85 g) plum, diced

1 medium (85 g) kiwifruit, diced

1 cup (250 g) almond milk, unsweetened

2 scoops (120 g) vanilla flavored ice cream

4 ice cubes

Method

1. Place the watermelon, plum, kiwi fruit, almond milk, ice cream, and ice cubes in a blender. Process until it becomes smooth.
2. Pour into 2 serving glasses. Garnish with a slice of watermelon or kiwi, if desired.
3. Serve and enjoy!

Nutritional Information:

Energy - 200 kcal, Fat – 9.7 g, Carbs - 27.2 g, Protein – 3.6 g, Sodium - 111 mg

-

Papaya Banana and Coconut Milkshake

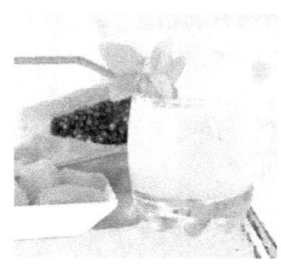

Preparation Time: **5 minutes**

Yield: 2 servings

Ingredients

8 ounces (250 g) frozen ripe papaya, diced

5 ounces (150 g) frozen banana, cut into small pieces

1/4 cup (60 ml) coconut milk

3/4 cup (185 ml) skim milk

4 ice cubes

Fresh mint sprigs

Method

1. Combine the papaya, banana, coconut milk, skim milk, and ice in a blender. Process until it becomes smooth.
2. Pour into 2 chilled glasses. Garnish with fresh mint sprigs.
3. Serve and enjoy!

Nutritional Information:

Energy - 198 kcal, Fat - 7.5 g, Carbs - 29.0 g, Protein - 5.7 g, Sodium - 76 mg

Avocado Honeydew Milkshake

Preparation Time: **5 minutes**

Yield: 2 servings

Ingredients

1/2 medium (100 g) avocado, stoned and diced

1 cup (170 g) honeydew melon

2 scoops (120 g) vanilla ice cream

1 cup (250 ml) low-fat milk

4 ice cubes

Method

1. Place the avocado, honeydew melon, ice cream, milk, and ice cubes in a high-speed blender. Process until smooth and creamy.
2. Pour into 2 chilled glasses. Garnish with a slice of avocado or melon, if desired.
3. Serve and enjoy.

Nutritional Information:

Energy - 257 kcal, Fat - 15.5 g, Carbs - 27.4 g, Protein - 4.0 g, Sodium - 146 mg

-

Vanilla Fig and Cashew Milkshake

Preparation Time: **5 minutes**

Yield: 2 servings

Ingredients

2 (65 g) figs, cut into small pieces

2 scoops (120 g) vanilla ice cream

2 tablespoons (15 g) cashew nuts

1 cup (250 ml) whole milk

4 ice cubes

Method

1. Combine the figs, vanilla ice cream, cashews, and milk in a blender. Process until it becomes smooth.
2. Pour mixture into 2 chilled glasses. Garnish with fig slices, if desired.
3. Serve and enjoy.

Nutritional Information:

Energy - 250 kcal, Fat - 11.1 g, Carbs - 29.6 g, Protein - 7.8 g, Sodium - 120 mg

-

-

Rich Chocolate Milkshake

Preparation Time: **5 minutes**

Yield: 2 servings

Ingredients

2 scoops (120 g) chocolate ice cream

1/4 cup (80 g) dark chocolate sauce

1 cup (250 ml) whole milk

6 ice cubes

Cocoa powder

Method

1. Place the chocolate ice cream, chocolate sauce, milk, and ice in a high-speed blender. Process until smooth and creamy.
2. Pour into 2 chilled glasses. Sprinkle with cocoa powder, if desired.
3. Serve and enjoy.

Nutritional Information:

Energy - 257 kcal, Fat - 7.4 g, Carbs - 40.8 g,
Protein - 7.1 g, Sodium - 129 mg

-

-

Pumpkin Pie Milkshake

Preparation Time: **5 minutes**

Yield: 2 servings

Ingredients

3/4 cup (185 g) pumpkin puree

2 scoops (120 g) vanilla ice cream

1 tablespoon (7 g) chopped walnuts

1/4 teaspoon (0.5 g) pumpkin pie spice

1 cup (250 ml) almond milk, unsweetened

Pumpkin seeds, for garnish (optional)

Method

1. Combine the pumpkin puree, vanilla ice cream, walnuts, pumpkin pie spice, and almond milk in a blender. Process until it becomes smooth.
2. Pour mixture into 2 chilled glasses. Garnish with some pumpkin seeds, if desired.
3. Serve and enjoy!

Nutritional Information:

Energy - 224 kcal, Fat - 13.5 g, Carbs - 22.6 g, Protein - 4.7 g, Sodium - 131 mg

Raspberry and Pear Milkshake

Preparation Time: **5 minutes**

Yield: 2 servings

Ingredients

1 cup (250 g) frozen raspberries, plus more for garnish

1 medium (180 g) pear, peeled, cored and cut into small pieces

2 scoops (120 g) vanilla ice cream

1 cup (250 ml) skim milk

Fresh mint sprigs

Method

1. Combine the raspberries, pear, vanilla ice cream, and milk in a blender. Process until it becomes smooth.
2. Pour mixture into 2 chilled glasses. Garnish with some raspberries and mint sprigs.
3. Serve and enjoy.

Nutritional Information:

Energy - 257 kcal, Fat - 7.6 g, Carbs - 41.1 g, Protein - 7.6 g, Sodium - 119 mg

Creamy Banana Soy Milkshake

Preparation Time: **5 minutes**

Yield: 2 servings

Ingredients

2 frozen bananas (about 150 g each), cut into small pieces

2 scoops (120 g) vanilla flavored ice cream

1 cup (250 g) soy milk

1/4 teaspoon (0.5 g) ground cinnamon

Method

1. Combine the banana, ice cream, soy milk, and cinnamon in a high-speed blender. Process until smooth and creamy.
2. Pour into 2 chilled glasses.
3. Serve and enjoy.

Nutritional Information:

Energy - 306 kcal, Fat - 11.5 g, Carbs - 45.1 g, Protein - 7.8 g, Sodium - 99 mg

Luscious Strawberry Milkshake

Preparation Time: **5 minutes**

Yield: 2 servings

Ingredients

1 cup (220 g) frozen strawberries, hulled and halved

2 scoops (120 g) vanilla ice cream

2 tablespoons (30 ml) strawberry syrup

1 cup (250 g) skim milk

Method

1. Combine the strawberries, vanilla ice cream, strawberry syrup, and milk in a blender. Process until it becomes smooth.
2. Pour mixture into 2 chilled glasses.
3. Drizzle with strawberry syrup on top to decorate (optional).
4. Serve and enjoy.

Nutritional Information:

Energy - 259 kcal, Fat - 7.0 g, Carbs - 41.5 g, Protein - 6.3 g, Sodium - 118 mg

Vanilla Apricot and Banana Milkshake

Preparation Time: **5 minutes**

Yield: 2 servings

Ingredients

1 cup (165 g) frozen apricots, stoned

1 large (180 g) frozen banana, sliced

1 scoop (60 g) vanilla ice cream

1 cup (250 ml) low-fat milk

Fresh mint sprig

Method

1. Combine the apricots, banana, vanilla ice cream, and milk in a high-speed blender. Process until smooth and creamy.
2. Pour into 2 chilled glasses. Garnish with apricot slices, if desired.
3. Serve and enjoy.

Nutritional Information:

Energy - 225 kcal, Fat - 8.7 g, Carbs - 30.6 g, Protein - 7.4 g, Sodium - 111 mg

Blueberry Cheesecake Milkshake

Preparation Time: **5 minutes**

Yield: 2 servings

Ingredients

1 cup (155 g) frozen blueberries

1/2 cup (110 g) mascarpone cheese

1 scoop (60 g) vanilla ice cream

1 cup (250 ml) low-fat milk

1 tablespoon (20 g) agave nectar or honey

Method

1. Combine the blueberries, mascarpone, vanilla ice cream, milk, and agave nectar in a blender. Process until it becomes smooth.
2. Pour mixture into 2 chilled glasses. Garnish with some blueberries, if desired.
3. Serve and enjoy.

Nutritional Information:

Energy - 242 kcal, Fat - 6.0 g, Carbs - 34.6 g, Protein - 13.6 g, Sodium - 210 mg